pear

carly johnson

this one's for you, pear.

re: choices

people say love is a choice,
but love is not a choice.
I do not choose to love you.
It would be impossible to choose not to.

table of contents

falling

pear

I found you when I gave up searching.

my flashlight flickered off.
my glasses lost their lens.
my baggage abandoned in transit.
and there you were.

slow, then all at once.

that's how I fell for you.
one day we were walking, distance between us.
the next, I felt your fingers brush against mine.
and then all of a sudden, I couldn't imagine
a world where you weren't by my side.

I thought I'd never be happier than that day on the mountain,
feeding wild goats with you,
but you showed me every day that's our day
is the happiest day of my life.

pear

I saw a couple awkwardly holding hands,
fingers fidgeting,
glances shy,
and I smile, remembering the first time you held mine.

Smoke occupied our lungs,
until our laughter turned into coughs.
you lifted your hand to measure against mine
and when you did, our fingers intertwined.

The truth is I'm dating her,
but I'm falling for you.

When I close my eyes,
it's not her I picture,
it's you.

I picture your goofy bucket hats,
your fish shirt,
your smile,
I hear your laugh in the deepest chamber of my heart.

The truth is
it's You I want.

johnson

You told me you didn't want to interfere,
but I told you I needed you to,
so you did,
and I'm forever grateful for that.

I'm glad you took a chance on me.
The she/they with the peeling nose
and the almost girlfriend back home.

You opened yourself up,
and you let me in.

I fell into you like a kid falls off their bike.
it's scary – the fall –
but I landed, soft, on the autumn leaves.

I fell for the way you scrunch your nose
when I call you beautiful.

I fell for the way your chuckles turn into snorts
when I tell a lackluster joke.

I fell for your "this is awesome"'s and your "thanks."

I fell for your frowns, for your grins,
and for everything in between.

A constant scribble
in my sketchbook
like a middle-schooler,
I draw your name with a heart.

pear

Greasy fingers,
buffalo sauce adorning your kissable lips,
your smile illuminated under the table light.

I've never seen anything cuter than the way
you devoured those chicken wings in Cairns.

johnson

Upholstered seats,
kernels decorating the aisles,
you spend more time
watching my reactions
than you do the screen.

The concrete is hard under my feet
but your hand is soft in mine.

A bridge made of wooden beams,
you wore my red lipstick proudly on your cheek.

I still remember the day Honey became a person.

No longer food for the bears,
Honey became You.

One day we were eating charcuterie on a rooftop.
The 'cheese' melted in our mouths,
I told you it was rich people cheese
but it turns out

it was just butter.

There's no one I'd rather eat a pound of butter with than you.

pear

I learned I'm not a puzzle that needs completion.
I am whole on my own.
You are not my missing piece, my other half.
You are my partner, my equal.

Your freckles are a roadmap to our love.
I get on the train and follow its path to your heart.

loving

L-o-v-e.
Love.
Love is a funny word.
I spent so much time thinking I didn't understand it,
and then I met You.

I thought love was a rollercoaster —
with sudden twists and turns.
One minute you're on the Mine Train,
and the next it's Kingda Ka.
But You, You taught me that's not true.

Love is the breeze in the summer,
hot chocolate in the snow,
an umbrella in a storm.

Love is You.

You taste of chocolate after a long day.
Your scent is of pine,
Your touch, the softest cloud.
The sight of you makes my heart flutter,
each time you giggle, I yearn to hear your laugh once more.

johnson

You tell me
you care about me severely.
I tell you,
I'm in love with you too.

pear

Someone once told me
if freckles are heart-shaped kisses left by your soulmate,
I was very loved in a past life.

I tell them,
I'm very loved in this one too.

Loving you is a gift.
On your best
and on your worst days,
you're my favorite gift to unwrap.

pimple patches,
peeling skin,
sunburn,
scaly legs,
unshaved armpits.

i tell you i'm a disaster,
and you tell me,
you've never seen anyone more beautiful.

~~I wonder~~
No, I know it to be true
that in each life our fates intertwine.
There's not a single universe
where your eyes don't smile into mine.

You're my sun, my moon, and my stars.

johnson

Even when I wake you up way before reality begins,
when my breath smells of acid and mornings,
you get so giddy when I kiss you.

pear

Sometimes I don't recognize the knots in my neck,
the tension in my shoulders
the ache in my feet,
until you hold me, and I melt into you.

With you, I'm no longer complex.
I am simply a warm blanket,
and that's all I need to be.

pear

I once got so high I forgot the color purple existed,
but even then,
I could never forget our love.

Flowers no longer belong in a garden
but in a vase
for You.

they say there has to be one person who kills the bugs,
but I say that's simply not true.

I love the way you save these little creatures too.

johnson

Sometimes our beloved window unit
isn't enough to fight off the summer heat
but you never get too warm to hold me.

Butterflies still flutter,
my palms still sweat,
my heart still races,
each time I see you.

I want you to know

I love your fit checks,
your nap hair,
your little tattoo,
your rosy cheeks,
your nose scrunches,
your striped button down,
your shoe obsession,
your stomach,
your thighs,
your lips,
your eyes,
I Love You.

pear

I love how you can never hold in a surprise.

Your excitement overtakes you like a Bondi current,
sweeps you under the surf,
until you burst like a confetti-filled balloon.

When I lay in bed with you,
the lights may be on
but the world is turned off.

There is nothing but your arm around me
and your sweet kiss.

In your embrace, I am safe.
In your smile,
In your arms,
In your future,
and in mine,
I am safe.

It's an honor to do this with you.

You're my flora.
A precious sunflower.
Chin lifted toward the light.

johnson

I run my fingers through your hair,
my hand caresses your cheek,
your eyes tell me words your mouth need not share,
you kiss my forehead and I know
you love me too.

pear

Picasso on the wall,
Rembrandt,
Monet.

But no painting gathers a crowd quite like You.

Never stop
throwing your head back laughing at my mediocre jokes.

Never stop
holding me when I'm fast asleep.

Never stop
twirling my hair around your fingers.

Never stop loving me.

Hold my hand
through the subway turnstile.

Hold my hand
through the summer heat.

Hold my hand
through the tough times.

Hold my hand
through the best days.

We had a fight today,
and it nearly broke us.

I nearly threw it all away
but then I remembered our vow.

No matter how hard it gets,
we always end each night with
I love you.

longing

Fairway Lane

There's nothing *fair* about the *way*
the universe keeps me from you
this month of May.

I miss your laugh,
your honeycomb glasses,
your curves,
I miss you.

We're 260 miles apart,
but somehow,
you never make me feel alone.

pear

No matter how far,
we live under the same sky.

I look to the stars
and I know,
you're looking up at the same ones.

If I were a building,
I'd always leave a window cracked for you
so even on your worst nights,
you could always find your way home.

pear

We say long distance is good for us,
it allows us to find ourselves, to be ourselves,
but it hurts like hell not having you here.

28:12:36:02

We count down the days
        the hours
        the minutes
        the seconds
        until we see each other again.

The train was especially loud that day,
but not loud enough to conceal our love.

I love you is not a secret.
Nor a whisper.

I love you is shouted from the highest rooftop.
Your throat hurts and your voice cracks
but you never stop yelling.

The bed is so empty
without your baggy t-shirt
and the socks you can't sleep without.

When I fall asleep,
I imagine you're here
holding me.

pear

I surround myself in pretty words
but there's no poetry
as beautiful as you.

they always say we're so lucky to have found each other
but there's no luck in destiny.

You and I.
We're meant to be.

Destiny is a series of small moments.
A trail of breadcrumbs that all lead to you.

Grant me one wish tonight,
and I'd wish for you.

Your kisses are the sunset,
Your eyes the palms.
Your smile the seagulls,
Your laugh the waves.

Dream of me tonight my love.
dream of me on the shore,
my hair unkept,
blue as the sea.

for you darkest moments:

my love,
let your tears fall.
you're beautiful.
you're wise.
your humor feeds villages.
your love lights a dark room.
I will never tire of you.

send your deepest troubles my way.
allow me to kiss them out of you.
to bury them deep.
where they'll soon be forgotten.

give me your scars.
give me your trauma.
give me your heartache.

give it all to me,
and I'll shelter the weight.

you cry when you miss me,
when you know you're going to miss me soon,
when you love me so much you can't hold it in,

I know they told you it's a weakness,
so you say you're not emotional,
but I love this part of you.

pear

It's easy to love someone when
your toes are in the sand and daiquiris are aplenty,
but there's something to be said about loving someone
between appointments and bodega runs.

johnson

I've seen the northern lights,
I've toured the opera house,
I've danced under starlit skies,
but I've never felt happier than
on a lazy Sunday morning with you.

pear

Touring apartments together,
they said we could see the statue of liberty from the balcony,
but all I could see was our future.

I hope you savor these words I write for you,
crumple them up,
put them in a jar,
and close the lid so they don't escape.

Savor them and their sweet taste
for the days you need them most.

Love me like your favorite book.
Read me over and over again.

Pluck me from your garden,
press me between two paper weights,
and frame me beside your favorite print.

desiring

can I kiss you?

This night, our room was just ours.
We watched darts –
I'm sure they think it's a cover, but it's true.

We watched darts until I turned to face you.
I feel butterflies even now thinking of the first time I asked,

once upon a time we were roommates.
you walked around our room in your lace bralette,
and i couldn't breathe.

I loved when you got jealous.
Before you and i were a You and I,
they hit on me —
endlessly —
and you hated it
but I loved watching you hate it.

Your eyes are the prettiest ivy I've ever seen.
In bloom, year-round.

pear

My heart beats so fast when you come near.
I feel if it fluttered any quicker, I'd find myself
lifted

off the ground.

I catch your eye, watching your face move down my body,
your lips trailing every inch of my skin.

I feel your breath between my thighs,
your kiss on my heart-shaped tattoo.

I imagine
rain soaking through our white t-shirts,
our broken umbrella rendered useless in the storm.

I imagine
you lift my arms above my head,
holding them there in one hand.

I imagine
you nudge your knee between my thighs,
and your lips find mine.

Kiss me in a blizzard.
My fingers ice, your touch my salvation.
Pull me close, and don't ever let go.

Kiss me in a hurricane.
My feet swept away, your lips my life vest.
Pull me close, and don't ever let go.

There are so many words to choose from.
171,476 to be exact.

But when I see you in that tank top,
I forget them all.

johnson

Grab my hand and lead the way.
Undo my corset and kiss me slow.
You're my queen, and I love you so.

Kiss stories into my skin.
Draw the mona lisa with your touch.

I grab your hand and pull you close.
and suddenly,
we're the only people in the bar.
Your kisses are the only thing I feel,
your breath the only thing I hear,
all I need is the feeling of your body
pressed against mine
pressed against the wall.

Fishnets.
Thigh-highs.
We linger in the stall.

We're walking under billboard lights,
you're wearing a black blazer,
and your bralette – god I'm so in love.

Midnight kisses are one thing
but I live for your hands all over me at 3pm.

You tell me
one day
when we have enough money
to afford a kitchen counter
it won't be for cutting vegetables.

pear

I feel your love in every centimeter of my body.

I melt into you.

Beside you at a park,
filled with alcohol and desire,
a Tuesday night that crept into a Wednesday dawn,
I was grateful the button of your shorts was easy to undo.

johnson

Your finger through the loop of my jeans,
you pull me close and kiss me
on a busy brooklyn street.

Kiss me softly in the spots hardened by lovers past.

Thank you for always asking me
for parts of me
others thought belonged to them.

You're beautiful in your work uniform,
your wedding suit,
your swim trunks,
your pjs,
god I can't get enough of you.

My favorite time to kiss you isn't
when your hair is brushed, and your shirt buttoned.

My favorite time to kiss you is
when your eyes first taste the light of day,
your mouth first opens, your lips dry in the cool air.

You taste of sleep, peace, comfort,
and all that's good in the world.

Your eyes glance down at my lips
then back up again.
I lean in, ever so slightly,

in that tension
I find my favorite moment.

The arch of your back
is my bridge.
I swim under it and don't dare come up for air.

Kiss my neck.
My shoulders.
My ribs.
My stomach.

Your touch lifts the hairs on my arms,
leaves goosebumps in its wake.

pear

I wake to your arms around me.
your breath on my skin.
your body against mine.

johnson

Keep the lights on.

Love me slow.
Fast.
Then slow again.

Let me hear your love.

Carve your name into my skin.

And please,

don't ever forget how breathtaking you are.

dreaming

pear

they tell me to be careful,
that I'm your first love and may not be your last,
but I don't doubt you'll love me forever.

they tell me movies are made-up, an unachievable fantasy,
but dancing around the kitchen,
I know I've found my movie with you.

The only cold feet I have are
the ones I tuck between your legs
for you to warm up.

Airlie Beach,
Townsville,
Sydney,
Cairns,
Rotorua,
Auckland,
Dallas,
New York City,
Paramus,
Frederick,
I've kissed you in so many cities,
and I can't wait to kiss you in so many more.

pear

You look at me like you've never seen anything so beautiful,
like you've never known this feeling before,
like you never thought it possible,
and I know this
because I feel it too.

Our dates encroach into tomorrow
and the next day
and the day after that
until your toothbrush finds its home beside mine.

Two toothbrushes.
Two towels.
Two hearts and twenty toes.

I'll steal your clothes,
and you'll steal mine.

pear

You tell me you'll bake chocolate chip cookies
(and lift your shirt for me)
on the days that are too much to bare.

I tell you no day with you could be too much to bare,
(but I also wouldn't mind.)

Eternity with you will never be enough.
no matter how hard it gets,
I will never have enough of you.

pear

I'll love you til my dying breath
and even after that,
I'll find a home among the stars
to shine my love down upon you.

I dream of a day when out of the corner of my eye,
I see a sparkle on your finger.

For the first time in my life,
I'd give up my last name.

We should practice our wedding kiss.

Will you dip me in our first dance?

johnson

I haven't told you this yet
but one day,
I hope we buy matching pj sets
for us
and for our little ones.

pear

Our kids will never know a household without love.

I loved you yesterday
I love you today,
I'll love you tomorrow.

they say,
take a picture,
it'll last longer,
but nothing will last longer than our love.

I'm grateful we were born when we were.
because in another time,
your lips wouldn't find mine in the daylight.
Our love would be etched into letters,
hidden in dresser drawers.
I'd love you between the socks and stockings,
and no one would know.

pear

I'm grateful for the light that sneaks into our city studio,
caressing the side of your face
until I awake, and my hand takes its place.

Thank you for the forehead kisses
you sneak in the middle of the night.

Thank you for the cuddles
you give even in the Australian summer.

Thank you for the reassurance on the days I need it most.

Thank you for the privilege to love you, forever and always.

Made in the USA
Coppell, TX
15 June 2023

18144861R00085